learning
for earning

ERIC PARSLOE AND
CAROLINE ALLEN

Eric Parsloe is the director of the Oxford School of Coaching and Mentoring and the author of several books on maximising individual potential and performance. In the 1970s he founded the Epic Group, an employee communication and multimedia company (now the largest multimedia learning production company in the UK). He was chairman of the multimedia industry body BIMA and is currently chairman of the Centre for International Debate and Communication Training at the English Speaking Union. He is also a qualified rugby coach.

Caroline Allen is a director of the No-Nonsense Team Ltd, which specialises in individual and team development, coaching senior executives and their teams in how to meet both personal and organisational goals. Qualified in social psychology and organisational development, she has experience of both the public and private sectors from her work in the Cabinet Office and as the human resources development manager for GlaxoWellcome. She is an external examiner for the Oxford School of Coaching and Mentoring, and lives in Buckinghamshire with her husband, Richard, and their boxer dog, Hobbes.

Management Shapers is a comprehensive series covering all the crucial management skill areas. Each book includes the key issues, helpful starting points and practical advice in a concise and lively style. Together, they form an accessible library reflecting current best practice – ideal for study or quick reference.

BROMLEY COLLEGE

of Further & Higher Education

The Institute of Personnel and Development is the leading publisher of books and reports for personnel and training professionals, students, and all those concerned with the effective management and development of people at work. For full details of all our titles please contact the Publishing Department:

tel. 0181-263 3387
fax 0181-263 3850
e-mail publish@ipd.co.uk

The catalogue of all IPD titles can be viewed on the IPD website:
http://www.ipd.co.uk

learning
for earning

ERIC PARSLOE AND
CAROLINE ALLEN

INSTITUTE OF PERSONNEL AND DEVELOPMENT

Design by Curve
Typesetting by Paperweight
Printed in Great Britain by
The Guernsey Press, Channel Islands

British Library Cataloguing in Publication Data
A catalogue record for this book is available from the
British Library

ISBN
0-85292-774-6

The views expressed in this book are the authors' own and
may not necessarily reflect those of the IPD.

**INSTITUTE OF PERSONNEL
AND DEVELOPMENT**

IPD House, Camp Road, London SW19 4UX
Tel.: 0181 971 9000 Fax: 0181 263 3333
Registered office as above. Registered Charity No. 1038333.
A company limited by guarantee. Registered in England No. 2931892.

contents

acknowledgements

No book is ever produced without the help and encouragement of colleagues, friends, partners and family. That is certainly true of this book, and the authors wish to acknowledge the contributions they have received with their grateful thanks and appreciation.

Other titles in the series:

introduction

'Learning for earning' is a catchy way of summarising an awkward fact about the modern world.

In the 1950s, 1960s and early 1970s it was acceptable to treat 'learning' as something you did at school or college and then left behind you as you entered the world of work. Beyond this, and certainly once you had learned your basic trade or served your 'professional apprenticeship', learning was not a habit that applied to the adult world.

But in the 1980s and 1990s the world of work changed – in some ways beyond recognition. Experts predict that the rate of change will continue to increase. Things that were once produced in Birmingham can now be equally well produced in most countries around the world – and often more quickly and cheaply. By the time you have mastered the latest computer program, a new, better and cheaper version has been produced in Brazil, Brisbane or Barcelona. So you have to start learning all over again.

Today, learning is not an option. If you want to maintain the earning power you already have, let alone earn more, then learning is a necessity. If you want to *return* to work after a break, or have the misfortune to be forced to find a new job or career, then the need to learn is an even higher priority.

In this book we have shared our experiences of 'learning for earning'. We have included techniques and suggestions that we know have worked effectively for others. Not all of them will suit you, but you should try them before you discard them. You need to take control of your own learning – because no one else will – and this book is a way of starting that process.

Our ideas and suggestions are structured as follows:

● First, you need to be sure that 'learning for earning' is really important to you at this point in your life. If it is, then you can reflect, in a broad-brush way, on the things that are important to you for your life-style ambitions and goals.

■ Having decided how relevant learning is to you, you can begin to analyse where you are starting from. What are your *existing* strengths and abilities, and what type of person are you — or what could you be?

▲ Next we suggest you begin to think quite differently about the challenges and opportunities that face you, because 'conventional thinking' may hold you back.

● The process you will then have followed will help you recognise the very wide range of development options available to you. But you now need to understand which of those options are most likely to suit your natural learning preferences.

● Next you need to understand that the responsibility for making all this learning happen lies with you, and here we offer some ideas.

● The key to success is accepting that you need not be on your own. A great deal of help is available, so self-responsibility does not mean solo-responsibility. We advocate that the key to success can lie in helping someone else to learn simultaneously and to accept that *success comes most surely from learning how to do simple things consistently.*

We have set out to make this book an 'active read' by including practical, interactive exercises alongside the theory and general advice, so you will find it useful to have a pencil and some paper to hand. There are three types of exercise:

● **Activities.** These are mostly self-assessments or check-lists. They will provide you with interesting analyses of your situation as well as data for better decision-making. They will help you to focus on the core of your issues.

■ **Reflection points.** These are an opportunity for you to reflect on what you have been reading and make notes on how this relates to your own situation. Sometimes the questions posed may stimulate you to reflect more broadly on the topic in hand. You may also like to make a note of the *promises you make to yourself* about actions you intend to take as a result of what you have been reading.

▲ **Network help-line.** This is the final chapter, where we point you in the direction of other people, organisations or publishers who can provide more information and advice on the topics covered in this book. Although we cannot provide all the answers we can suggest where to find the specific help that you need.

This book is not written primarily for those who are already experienced learners, although we hope it will give you some new ideas, as well as reminding you of the basics. Our main aim is to help those of you who want to start to learn to ensure that you are in the best possible position to earn whatever you need for the material life-style you choose. But, of course, life is not all about work and money. It is also about emotional and spiritual fulfilment, and certainly about enjoyment and relaxation. So we have tried to keep it light and easy without detracting from the seriousness of the issues.

We both believe strongly in the value of receiving feedback, so we would love to hear in what ways this book has been helpful to you.

1 the importance of keeping pace

Anyone who stops learning is old, whether at twenty or eighty. Anyone who keeps learning stays young. The greatest thing in life is to keep your mind young.

Henry Ford

The fact that you have bothered to open this book suggests you think that, judging from the title, there would be some benefit to you in reading it. But what will you get from reading this book?

We suggest you begin to answer this question for yourself by spending a few moments completing the following self-assessment activity.

Activity 1   Assess yourself

Here are 10 questions to which you may answer either yes or no. Don't spend too long on each one agonising over whether the words exactly capture your feelings. These types of exercise are designed to give you a more accurate analysis, the more quickly you respond.

Q1   Did you gain your qualifications more than five years ago?

Q2   Would you like to change to a more flexible way of working?

Q3   Could you improve your current communication-technology skills?

Q4   Can you see yourself working simultaneously for more than one employer, client or customer in the next three years?

Q5   Do you definitely need to continue to work to maintain an acceptable life-style?

Q6   Do you, or your customers, need to compete internationally?

Q7   Are you likely to need new skills and knowledge to do the job of your choice in three years' time?

Q8   Is it possible that your organisation, or any of your customers' organisations, could be taken over or merged in the near future?

Q9   Would you like to become more independent in the way that you work?

Q10   Is there another job you would rather be doing in order to earn a living?

Now count up the number of statements to which you have answered yes. If there are, say, 5 out of 10, then we suggest that there is at least a 50 per cent chance that you will gain from reading this entire book.

If you have decided to read on, we are delighted. Learning to learn is one of the most important issues that you could choose to tackle. We believe also that simple but meaningful self-assessments can be a useful way of focusing on issues and producing information that can help you make more informed decisions.

The 10 statements we asked you to consider are not by any means all the aspects that need to be discussed. They were intended simply to start you thinking in terms of your immediate self-interest as well as the range of choices that you are faced with about your future direction.

The broader picture – for society

As we were putting the finishing touches to this book, a document entitled *Declaration on Learning* was published by eight of the UK's leading thinkers and writers on this subject. The *Declaration* proposes a list of no fewer than 14 major benefits of taking learning seriously. Those that we feel are particularly relevant to this book can be divided into two kinds: benefits for the individual, and benefits for society.

Benefits for the individual

- Learning is the key to developing a person's potential.

- Learning to learn is the key to effective learning.

- Learning enables the individual to meet the demands of change.

- The capacity to learn is an asset that never becomes obsolete.

Benefits for society

- Society survives and thrives through learning.

- A focus on capturing and sharing learning contributes to a more cohesive society.

▲ Learning helps to enhance the capacity of individuals to create a more fulfilled society.

These are the views of people with considerable experience in the field of learning, and we recommend you reflect on their views. The theme of balancing your own interests with those of others in your community is one we shall continue to explore in this book. It is important also to place your own concerns in the wider context of changes that are affecting people in all walks of life in many different parts of the world.

In recent years there have been literally thousands of articles written and speeches made on the link between learning and the need to cope with the challenges of the rapid changes in the world of work. One writer, Margaret Malpas, caught the prevailing mood well when she wrote of her experiences in Russia, Brunei, the Caribbean and Eastern Europe, where she tried to help whole nations and organisations (*and of course the individuals that make up these organisations*) accelerate their pace of 'catching up'. She believed that to accelerate the pace of learning there were three absolute prerequisites:

> The first is *vision* – the ability to be sensitive to small
> clues and synthesise them – in order to plan for as much
> of the future as can possibly be predicted. Short-termism
> is the antithesis in this respect.

Second, there has to be *solid commitment* by the organisation to real change as opposed to an illusion of achievement.

Third, *an exacting analysis of the priority of learning needs* must underpin the subsequent learning process.

What Malpas advocates as essential for whole economies and organisations we believe applies equally to individuals such as yourself as you begin to make your choices. None of us exists in isolation from the world around us.

The broader picture – for you

So what is the next step? There is a real danger that any plan for your learning that you draw up in a hurry will concentrate only on the types of jobs that you think might be available *now* and that might suit your existing knowledge and skills 'toolkit'. This is short-termism. It is important, if you are going to spend time to build up a well-thought-out plan, that you start by thinking in broad-brush terms about the whole range of things that you might do or become.

Fitting your future work into your real life-style goals and ambitions (the things that really seem important and valuable to you) is critical if you want to achieve genuine motivation at work and live a 'stress-free' life at the same time. So we suggest you try this next activity.

Activity 2   Your life-style goals

This activity simply suggests that you think for a while about each of the following questions and then note down your answers. You might need to set some time aside in a place where you are unlikely to be rushed or interrupted.

- ⊙ What are the hobbies and interests that you enjoy most?
- ▢ What are your main hopes and ambitions for your family?
- △ What are the key relationships that you would like to keep in the years ahead?
- ⊙ What are your strongest preferences and ambitions for your life at work?
- ⊙ If you had the choice, where would you prefer both to live and to work? Would it be to work from home or possibly abroad?
- ⊙ What social, charitable or community activities would you like to take part in?
- ▢ Apart from your hobbies, what are your wildest leisure preferences or ambitions — to travel, climb Everest, sunbathe on a desert island, conduct a symphony orchestra, or just curl up with a good book and a bottle of wine?

Having answered these questions honestly, now rate each of them on a scale of 1-10 where 10 = 'extremely important to me' and 1 = 'nice, but not very important to me'.

This activity is intended to encourage you to think widely and imaginatively about the choices you could make. Placing these hopes and dreams in an order of priority should have given you a simple scale of your order of 'real' priorities.

You should now have a clearer picture of what is important to you and what you might want to achieve, as well as the type of jobs that may give you the best chance of a satisfying and fulfilled life.

Reflection point

We suggest you pause for a moment to make a note of the main thoughts about your future that have occurred to you as a result of reading so far.

Is there something you feel you would like to do for your learning? If the answer is yes, then why not write down when you will start and by when you hope to have completed it? Of course, nobody but you need know, so don't fool yourself. Write it down only if you really intend to do it.

2 start from where you are

An unexamined life is not worth living.

Socrates

There is an old Irish story about the tourist who gets completely lost in rural Ireland. Eventually he meets a local farmer and asks, 'Could you please tell me the way to Dublin?' The farmer replies, 'Ah, to be sure, if I wanted to go to Dublin I wouldn't start from here!'

The relevance of this story to your own journey of learning and development is that *the direction you need to take will be determined very largely by the position you are starting from.* It therefore makes sense to spend a good deal of time establishing that accurately before leaping into action.

One way of summarising your current position is to draw up a conventional curriculum vitae (CV) containing details of your educational and professional qualifications and your career history to date. A CV that highlights your achievements in each of your jobs as well as the skills learnt is even more useful. But it is possible to build an even fuller personal databank by using a range of self-assessment techniques. We suggest you now try two activities. Activity

3 will help you take a pragmatic view of your current skills. Activity 4 will start to give you some insights into your personal preferences about work. For those interested in exploring their personality preferences and drives in more depth, we briefly discuss a further technique and point you in the direction of additional help.

So where are you now?

Remember that we said in the Introduction that not all activities will suit everyone, so feel free to skip to the next chapter at any time. We do, however, suggest you do the following activity.

Activity 3   Your 'skills tool-kit'

Use the following check-list to assess the skills that you feel you already have and those that you think it might be useful to develop. By the time you have finished this activity you will have some key information to help you make decisions on the direction your learning journey needs to take.

Work through each of the following skills and abilities and place a tick in the appropriate box, using the following key.

Key

Strength	= This is an area of strength for me.
Inconsistency	= Occasionally this can cause me some difficulty.
Need help	= I am not confident with this at all.

	Strength	Inconsistency	Need help

Managing yourself

Stating your needs clearly

Asking for help and support

Feeling able to say no when
necessary

Setting yourself goals and
standards

Setting yourself deadlines

Accepting rejection

Asking for feedback on your
work and ideas

Making and using contacts

Concentrating

Making decisions

Taking risks

Gathering and assessing data
and facts

Playing with ideas and
building a vision

Giving a presentation

Understanding your feelings
and motivations

Dealing with the unexpected

Having fun

Managing others

Listening intently to the
views and opinions of
others

Delegating

Giving clear instructions

	Strength	Inconsistency	Need help
Giving constructive criticism			
Interviewing others			
Chairing meetings			
Helping others to develop			
Training or coaching			
Appreciating others' skills and contributions			
Dealing with the clients			
Empathising with others' situations and feelings			

Managing things

	Strength	Inconsistency	Need help
Reading quickly			
Keeping accurate records			
Using information technology			
Writing letters and reports			
Organising books, papers and files			
Preparing presentations			
Planning			
Preparing meetings			
Managing time effectively			

Now look back at your answers. Where are most of your 'Strengths'? Where are most of your 'Need help' areas? Are there any patterns to where your strengths or weaknesses lie? Which of the areas marked 'Inconsistency' and 'Need help' would you most like to develop? Would it help to prioritise these? Is it worth asking for another opinion? After all, sometimes we tend to be overcritical and at others we may be too complacent.

You should now have a sense of your priorities and a direction for your personal development from a practical starting-point. You will have considered the skills that you already have and begun to identify skills that you might usefully develop. But the practical view is only one dimension.

So what is your *preferred* way of operating?

The next activity will give you insights into the way that *you prefer to work*. Crucially, it will also allow you to appreciate the different preferences and approaches that other people have and which may conflict with your own. Working in an environment that meets your preferences and, at the same time, is balanced with the preferences of other colleagues is a desirable target at which to aim.

There are literally scores of tests available that will provide you with a picture of what kind of person you are and where your strengths and weaknesses in work situations might be. Traditionally, these kinds of test have been used by employers to help them fit people to the jobs that they wish to fill. But in the world of work today, as we have already indicated, employers will be taking a less active role in helping to equip you for the opportunities that are available. Employers will increasingly expect you to take responsibility for your future employability. It therefore makes good sense to use these techniques for your own purposes. For many of us, this may lead into unfamiliar but perhaps very revealing territory. This part of your learning journey can be one of the most valuable stages and help open your eyes to the wide range of possibilities that exist.

Activity 4 gives you just a taste of the techniques and questions used in personality-profiling. If this really is unfamiliar territory for you, then we strongly suggest you consult an experienced person to get more detailed information and advice before going much further. But this 'taster' will provide a useful guide to what you can expect.

Activity 4   Your personality characteristics

The Myers-Briggs Type Indicator® is one of the most widely used tests. It explores people's preferences for the ways they get and focus their energy; the ways they gather and take in information; the ways they make decisions; and the ways they organise their lives. Here are some sample questions that can be found on the Indicator and that will point you to where your preferences might lie.

Energy

1 In a large group, do you more often:

a introduce others
b get introduced?

If you answered a) you may have a preference for extroversion (E), preferring to focus on the outer world of people and things and to learn by talking and doing.

If you answered b) you may have a preference for introversion (I), preferring to focus on the inner world of ideas and experiences and to learn by reading and reflecting.

Information

2 Do you usually get along better with:

a imaginative people
b realistic people?

If you answered a) you may have a preference for intuition (N), and like to focus on possibilities, patterns and the future. You may prefer to take a conceptual and theoretical approach to learning. If you answered b) you may have a preference for sensing (S), preferring to focus on the present and information gained from your senses. You may prefer a practical and reality-based approach to learning.

Decisions

3 Do you usually:

a value sentiment more than logic
b value logic more than sentiment?

If you answered a) you may have a preference for feeling (F), and like to base your decisions primarily on values and subjective evaluation of person-centred concerns. Personal rapport with your tutor and the material you are studying may be particularly important to you.
If you answered b) you may have a preference for thinking (T), preferring to base decisions on logic and objective analysis of cause and effect. It may be particularly important that your tutor shows fairness and competence and encourages critical debate.

Organisation

4 Are you more successful at:

a dealing with the unexpected and seeing quickly what should be done

b following a carefully worked out plan?

If you answered a) you may have a preference for perceiving (P), and like a flexible and spontaneous approach, preferring to keep your options open. You probably prefer a learning environment that allows you to feel unconstrained in how you approach your learning assignments.

If you chose b) you may have a preference for judging (J), and like a planned, organised approach to life, preferring to have things settled. You probably prefer a learning environment that provides structure and clear deadlines and that allows you to work steadily through assignments.

The combination of your four chosen responses indicates your overall type preference. If you are a mathematician you may by now have worked out that there are 16 different possible types. The authors share three of the characteristics but differ on extrovert (E) and introvert (I). So, for example, we need to work hard at the balance of our discussions, because Es prefer to talk rather than listen and Is prefer to listen rather than talk. Both have their advantages and disadvantages, but it is knowing our preferences that enables us to communicate more effectively. The value of the Myers-Briggs Type Indicator® lies not only in helping you to recognise your own preferences but also in helping you to understand the preferences of others, and therefore how you can interact with them as effectively as possible.

The full test asks many more questions and therefore produces a very much fuller picture. As we have said, you will need expert help and guidance to use this test, so we suggest you use the Network Helpline (Chapter 7) for more information.

The previous two activities have given you an overview of your current strengths and weaknesses. For many people this will be sufficient new information to handle as part of your decision-making process about your development plan.

It is possible, if you wish, to go much, much deeper into the subject of personality. Although some readers may not want to, we recognise that others may; for their benefit the next section gives the 'flavour' of a further technique.

Enneagram techniques

There are many avenues that you could explore if you wished to delve more deeply into the subject of personality. The going may get tough, however, as you try to grasp the new concepts. But enneagram techniques offer one way to choose how you might develop if you just let your natural preferences take you in the direction that best suits your 'real' personality type.

The word 'enneagram' is derived from the Greek words *ennea*, meaning 'nine', and *gramma*, meaning 'a thing recorded (eg written or drawn)', as in 'diagram'. Enneagram theory suggests that everybody has one of nine basic personality types which can be plotted on different points on a circle. Each type is connected to other types. When lines are drawn between these types a pattern or symbol is produced which is identical with symbols found in drawings from antiquity.

Enneagram symbol showing direction of natural progression

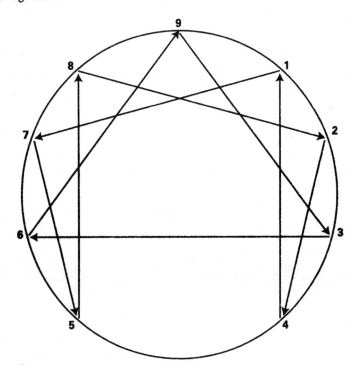

This leads to claims that the wisdom of enneagram techniques has been passed down through thousands of years. Others believe that it can be traced back no further than the Middle Ages, although its most certain origins are in the work of early-twentieth-century psychologists.

Whatever the origins, people who use the enneagram believe it gives deep insights into the essence of an individual's identity and can show their natural paths of development. Organisations as varied as the Vatican, the CIA and Motorola use the technique, demonstrating practical applications in the world of today.

According to the theory, people's personality types can be identified solely by their enneagram numbers, although some practitioners use titles as well. For instance, Don Risso uses 'The Leader' to describe number 8 and 'The Helper' to describe number 2. Each type has a further nine levels of characteristics within itself which are in turn divided into 'healthy state', 'average state' and 'unhealthy state'.

You can identify your own number and whether you are in a 'healthy', 'average' or 'unhealthy' state within that type simply by reading the enneagram descriptions and making your own decisions, although a questionnaire is also available. So in a sense you assess your own enneagram personality type.

The personality-type descriptions are brief but uncannily accurate. If you happen to be in an 'unhealthy state' it really can be a 'warts and all' experience. Most people find they are in an 'average state' but can then also clearly see what their characteristics would be if they were in a 'healthy state'. Progressing to a 'healthy' state provides a picture or goal for your natural development if you are prepared to allow the 'real you' to emerge.

If you want to find out more we suggest you read *Personality Types* by Don Risso and Russ Hudson (revised edition published in 1996 by Houghton Mifflin) or *The Enneagram* by Helen Palmer (published by Harper San Francisco in 1992). Risso and Hudson's book contains the detailed questionnaire.

The following is a brief summary of each Enneagram Personality Type, based mainly on the work of Risso and Hudson but with the labels used by Palmer also shown. At the end of each description there is the name of a famous person who Risso suggests may fit the type concerned – you can decide whether you think they fit the healthy descriptions!

Type 1 The Reformer or The Perfectionist
Rational, idealistic, perfectionist, self-righteous
Margaret Thatcher

Type 2 The Helper or The Giver
Nurturing, concerned, possessive, manipulative
Mother Theresa

Type 3   The Motivator or The Performer
Self-assured, adaptive, image-conscious, deceiver
Bill Clinton

Type 4   The Individualist or The Tragic Romantic
Intuitive, expressive, self-absorbed, depressive
Judy Garland

Type 5   The Investigator or The Observer
Perceptive, conceptualiser, detached, reclusive
Bill Gates

Type 6   The Loyalist or The Devil's Advocate
Endearing, responsive, evasive, paranoid
Princess Diana

Type 7   The Enthusiast or The Epicure
Enthusiastic, fun-loving, excessive, manic
Robin Williams

Type 8   The Leader or The Boss
Assertive, decisive, aggressive, ruthless
Saddam Hussein

Type 9   The Peacemaker or The Mediator
Receptive, supportive, self-effacing, dissociated
Ronald Reagan

These examples may all seem a little 'tongue in cheek'. But they give a flavour of the pictures that enneagram techniques paint for you. This certainly becomes much more revealing when you read, and reflect on, the full 'warts and all' descriptions of your own type.

There is an additional value in the exercise: being able to recognise that the 'natural path' of your development will flow not only within your type but also from one type to another along the following sequences:

● from Reformer to Enthusiast to Investigator to Leader to Helper to Individualist to Reformer

■ from Peacemaker to Motivator to Loyalist to Peacemaker.

Enneagram techniques also suggest that, under stress, people move in the opposite direction!

Once again we would emphasise that the enneagram technique is just one of many that will give you insights into the 'real' you; please also remember that you need to get expert help and advice if you want to explore such techniques further. You can find more information in the Network Helpline (Chapter 7).

The purpose of this chapter has been to help you get a much clearer and deeper picture of 'where you are starting from'. Some of the ideas may already have been familiar to you, others may not. Either way, your learning journey is going to require you to think in quite different and unfamiliar ways. That is the theme of the next chapter.

Reflection point

Once again we suggest you pause to think about the issues discussed in this chapter and how they may affect you. Is there something you feel you would like to commit to doing as soon as possible? If the answer is yes, then why not write down when you will start and the date by which you hope to have completed it? But write it down only if you really intend to do it!

3 now start thinking differently

People don't seem to realise that it takes time and effort and preparation to think. Statesmen, for instance, are far too busy making speeches to think.

Bertrand Russell

In this chapter we switch the focus to the way we *think* about learning and development. We shall suggest two activities. One will help you to start thinking differently about the *challenges* you are facing. The second will help you think about how you currently take *control* of the way you do things.

The way we were

Think back to the way you thought about learning in your schooldays. In a way it was quite easy. You arrived at the start of a new term with a rough idea of what subjects you were going to be taught and which class you were in. All you were required to do was turn up.

The rest was often not up to you because there was a national curriculum and someone else, more important and 'all-knowing', had already decided for you *what* it was you needed to learn. They had also decided *how* you were going to learn it, by *when*, with *whom* and to *what standard*. All that was required from you was to keep quiet, open your ears and get ready for learning to happen to you.

Well, of course, there was always a great debate about the usefulness of that traditional approach. But it was probably an effective method of ensuring that you at least knew a few facts, eg that Henry VIII had (among five others) a wife called Jane who didn't live too long.

Learning in this way did serve a purpose. You were being equipped to *pass exams* that tested your *knowledge* and occasionally your understanding of *known situations and facts*. Those were the days when you could learn something one year and, if necessary, come back the next and learn it again because the information you were learning was still relevant. The knowledge and facts required had hardly changed.

A similar story used to be true in the workplace, only here all you had to do was to go on a training course. Your employing organisation believed it knew that the product it was going to make or the service it would be providing tomorrow looked pretty much like the one it was making and providing today. It followed therefore that putting people on training courses where they could all learn how to do the same thing in the same way and at the same time made sense.

Today, life and learning are different mainly because the pace of change has increased. Some areas of our lives are changing so rapidly that by the time we have understood the change, they have changed again! The facts, information, skills, knowledge and understanding that we had last year may not be relevant to what we need to know today. The speed at which we learn therefore needs to increase at the same rate. If the pace of your learning is slower than the pace of change, you will become increasingly ill-equipped for the world in which you live. A similar thing happened to the dodo — and it became extinct. Some would argue that *only those whose pace of learning is faster than the pace of change* will be the real winners in the employment market of the future.

So what does all this mean to someone wanting to take responsibility for their own learning?

The language of learning

First of all we suggest that it means thinking differently about language.

Let's start with the words usually associated with learning. The fact is that 'training', 'development' and 'learning' are words that are often used interchangeably, as if they meant the same thing. This can make life confusing. We suggest that we need to be more careful with our choice of language:

● Typically, *training* more accurately describes the process used to enable someone to gain known skills, knowledge and sometimes behaviour. The process is usually owned by the organisation running the training, and the agenda is set by the trainer. There is usually a right and wrong way of doing things, and you can normally tick a box somewhere to say you have gained what was required.

■ *Development*, as a word, is more usually used in organisations to describe the process by which individuals make progress in developing their skills and knowledge and behaviours. Typically, people are expected, for example, to 'develop their competencies' or to 'develop up to the next grade'.

▲ *Learning*, on the other hand, is we believe more accurately defined *as both a process and as a continuous state of mind that transcends the boundaries and structures of organisations.* Of course, learning happens during the training and development processes. But it goes further than that.

You are as likely to be learning in the pub at 8 pm as you were in the office or factory at 3 pm. Learning is for life. It started the day you were born and, if you have the right attitude, it never stops. It is this learning process that you need to manage if you are to continue to earn money for as long as you choose, not for as long as someone else chooses.

If we were asked, 'What do you know today that you didn't know this time last year?' or 'What can you do today that you couldn't do last year?', most of us would possibly find it hard to answer very accurately. This is partly because we tend not to monitor our learning very effectively. It is also in part because we tend not to recognise readily when we are learning unless it is in a formal setting and labelled LEARNING. It is a little bit like Alice in Wonderland and the bottle labelled 'Drink Me'. Unless we are instructed to learn, we tend not to notice we have learned something. Not surprising, when all the traditional approach required was that we turn up and 'drink'.

So, in terms of the language we use we need to ban the phrase 'Learning means going on a training course.'

The language of our inner voice

There is another way in which language is important.

Although we may not always be aware of it, we 'talk to ourselves'. We do it all the time. And what we tell ourselves is what our minds believe. This is important when it comes to how you position learning for yourself. If you tell yourself that you *must* learn, or you *should* learn, or you *have to* learn, or you *ought to* learn, your subconscious will accept learning as a chore and something that gets in the way of other things that you would prefer to be doing.

Try to position anything you do regarding learning as something you positively *choose* to do: 'I choose to read', 'I choose to attend this workshop', 'I choose to learn.' The more you tell yourself that you choose to do something, the more you will feel in control of it. The more in control of it you feel, the greater the sense of personal satisfaction you will experience. Remember to think positively!

Consciously deciding to use different language will therefore help you also to think of different approaches that are more relevant to the world of work today.

Reflection point

How did you learn as a child? It is doubtful that your parents taped up your eyes and ears until set times of the day when they were ready to impart some fact into your head. It is much more likely that every minute of every waking hour you were absorbing, watching, talking, touching, experimenting, trying, failing and trying again, making connections, playing, listening etc.

You were, in fact, learning all the time. This is how learning needs to become for you again. Make a note of the last time you 'consciously or unconsciously learned' something new. Was it using the traditional approach? Could it have been done differently? Did it make you more, or less, eager to start learning again?

Thinking differently about knowledge and information

We have already discussed the new reality that, today, knowledge and information can become outdated and irrelevant very quickly. Something you knew to be true yesterday may not be true today. Also, it is becoming increasingly possible for *the many* to access knowledge and information traditionally held by *the few*. Thanks to the Internet many of us, for instance, could know what illness we are suffering from before we visit our doctors and, sometimes, could sort out the problem without bothering them at all. Similarly we can access our global competitors' brochures or visit their web-site to check their prices in just a few minutes on the computer.

So, learning *how to access knowledge and information* may be more important than learning the knowledge itself. Understanding the process may be more useful than trying to remember the facts.

Activity 5   Accessing information

You may find it useful to assess your current capability around accessing information. Go through each section simply answering yes or no.

Networks and contacts

- Do you have a sufficiently wide network of business and professional contacts?
- Do you actively set out to meet people who work in spheres different from your current network?
- Do you use social opportunities to broaden your range of professional acquaintances?
- Do you take the time to attend lectures and talks by organisations involved in your field of interest?

Information technology

- Are you really up to date with the information technology used in your profession or business environment?

- Have you become familiar with how much the Internet can do for you?

- Do you know how to use all of the features on your computer?

- If you have not used a computer recently, do you know where you can gain access to one?

- Do you know where you can go to learn how to make best use of IT?

General communication

- Do you read more than one daily newspaper regularly, including the business sections? (Did you know that it has been estimated that a single daily edition of *The Times* contains more information than was available in the whole lifetime of someone living in the seventeenth century?)

- Do you subscribe to more than one professional magazine or visit the web-sites of other publications?

- Do you know how to skip or speed-read?

- Do you actively select and listen to radio programmes or play information tapes on car journeys?

- Do you plan the week ahead to make sure you watch TV programmes in your field of interest?

The access points for knowledge and information are readily available to you (and, of course, to your competitors in the employment market). If you have answered no to more than two of these questions, you may be getting out of touch. If you have answered no to the information technology questions because you simply do not like computers, you are almost undoubtedly becoming rapidly out of touch.

Reflection point

Think carefully about the questions to which you answered no. Which of these would it be quite simple for you to do something about? Pick a couple and consider what action you could choose to take and by when.

Thinking differently about learning new skills

In Activity 3 you reviewed your current skills 'tool-kit' and the skills you thought you might need to develop. However, softer skills are likely to be at least as much use as, if not more than, the hard, tangible variety.

For example, in the future you are just as likely to need to learn how to move on very quickly from one situation to another as you are to use any type of equipment. Understanding how you should react in ambiguous situations, knowing how to cope with uncertainty, being able to act without clear instructions, dealing with issues at a moment's notice – all are examples of the kind of 'soft' skills you are likely to need in the workplace of the twenty-first century.

These are new challenges for many people. It is no longer enough to wait for someone else to alert you to the fact that you need to learn them. You are responsible for the skills you do or do not possess.

Thinking differently about who is in control

The difference between learning, training and development is very much about who is in control of the situation. How you approach your learning is likely to reflect the way you approach most things in your life. In this next activity, you have an opportunity to examine the extent to which you already take control of your life. Then we shall look at the implications of this for your learning.

Activity 6   Being in control

To gain some insight into your current level of control, go through the following questions answering yes or no.

- ⊙ I enjoy making things happen
- ◻ I often look towards the future
- △ I prefer to take control of events
- ⊙ I try to act in accordance with my personal beliefs and values
- ⊙ I know immediately when I am, or am not, committed to something
- ⊙ I like to make my own decisions
- ◻ I am very conscious of the 'here and now'.
- △ I enjoy making choices
- ⊙ I normally accomplish what I set out to achieve
- ⊙ I happen to life, life doesn't happen to me

People who answer yes to all of these questions are very much in control of their lives and moving in the direction they have chosen. They are likely to be content with what they are achieving and managing the stresses of life admirably. They are likely to be managing their learning in much the same way.

Have you answered no to any of these questions? If so, ask yourself *why* you answered no. What evidence can you point to that demonstrates that you behave in a way that has led you to say no? What are the implications of this behaviour for the way you are likely to manage your learning? Do you want to change this behaviour?

Reflection point

Spend some time working through these questions for each negative answer that you gave. Then jot down the answers you come up with and discuss with a coach, mentor, friend or colleague the alternative choices you have for behaving differently in each case.

The question of 'choice' is one of the keys to 'Learning for Earning'. The way you choose to react to the reality of future employability is up to you. It might seem a daunting and depressing task – or it may seem like a great opportunity. It depends which way you choose to think about it. If you recognise the need to learn, and develop a genuine desire to learn, you will have established the fundamental requirements for learning to occur.

You will certainly have begun to think differently about your future. You will also have given yourself the freedom to choose. We shall discuss this further in the next chapter.

4 choosing best options

There is no one right way to learn, since a match is needed between diverse opportunities and preferred learning styles.

Peter Honey *et al*, *Declaration on Learning*

We spent the last chapter discussing different ways of thinking and the ways you currently take control of things. We emphasised the importance of 'choosing' the approaches that you can take to learning, and we shall continue now with that theme.

Earlier we defined learning as 'both a process and a continuous state of mind that transcends the boundaries and structures of organisations'. We shall now look at this definition in more detail and relate it to the wide range of learning opportunities that this definition suggests are available.

'Easy' learning

Only a few lucky people find learning easy. One of the main reasons is that most of us have been used to being taught in pretty much the same standard way. We know that, given the chance, we prefer to choose to work in ways that suit us best. So, to make learning 'easier', why not choose to learn in ways that suit you best?

There is a great deal of research available on how adults learn best. Some writers suggest that there are three key questions you need to be able to answer to begin to understand what approach might suit you:

- How do you perceive information most easily: do you learn best by seeing, hearing, moving or touching?

- How do you organise and process the information you receive: are you predominantly left brain, right brain, analytical (reductive) or global (deductive)?

- What conditions are necessary to help you take in and store the information you are learning: the emotional, social, physical and environmental factors?

Other writers emphasise the differences in people's 'Learning Intelligences', or their ability to:

- speak and write well
- reason, calculate and handle logical thinking
- paint, take great photographs or create sculpture
- use their hands or body
- compose songs, sing or play musical instruments
- relate to others
- access their inner feelings.

Learning needs to match the way the brain works

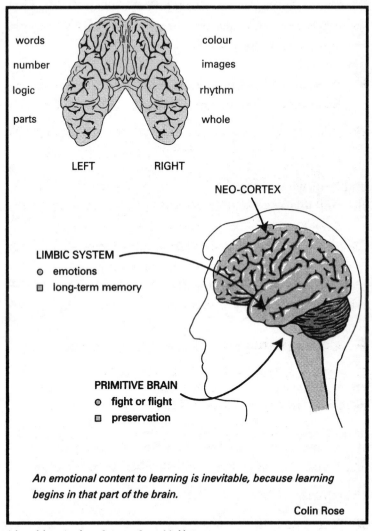

> *An emotional content to learning is inevitable, because learning begins in that part of the brain.*
>
> **Colin Rose**

Adapted from *Accelerate Learning*, Jenny Maddern

One writer, Jenny Maddern, has captured these ideas with her simple graphic in her booklet, *Accelerate Learning*, when she emphasises that learning needs to match the way the brain works (see the illustration on page 43).

Unfortunately, the traditional approach that many trainers and developers still use often fails to use our knowledge about how the brain works and the importance of the emotional aspects of learning. Some 'leading-edge' training is based on the acceptance that learning is more effective when, like children, we are brave enough to play games, tell stories, sing, tell jokes and set out to have fun while it is happening.

Of course, learning can be hard work. But as soon as you feel it is becoming boring as well then our advice would be to stop immediately. Go for a walk, put on a CD of lively music, go for a swim, do something you really enjoy. Then remind yourself of what you are trying to achieve and start again. You will be surprised at the difference in your learning progress. It is often said about learning that 'the more you enjoy it, the easier it becomes, the more you'll do it and the more you will remember it'.

If you want more information on the literature about *Accelerate Learning* you can use the Network Helpline (Chapter 7).

Learning preferences

Clearly, there is a wide range of variables to consider when you begin to think about how you might learn more easily. To help you identify the factors that apply most strongly to you, it might help to go back to part of our earlier definition of learning. We said that 'learning is both a process and a continuous state of mind'.

Considering learning as a *process* offers some valuable practical insights. Learning can be described as the process of acquiring new knowledge, understanding and skills. It is also believed to be a continuous cycle, and the diagram below illustrates how people learn from experience. The process has no beginning, middle or end. Depending upon the learning situation, people can enter the cycle at any time. The most effective learning, however, will take place when you have an opportunity to complete all the stages in the cycle (see diagram on page 46).

Everyone will find some stages in this learning cycle easier than others. Your preference for a particular stage in the continuous learning cycle reflects your preferred *learning style*. Recognising your own style, or combination of styles, will help you select learning opportunities that suit your style best. Equally importantly, learning-style analysis suggests what you may have to do to adjust your preferences to make the most of the learning opportunities that are actually available. Life does not always present us with options to do exactly what we choose.

The learning process

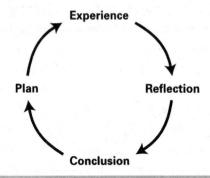

EXPERIENCE	This is the actual learning experience. It may be: **Reactive** – something which happens to you, or **Proactive** – an experience which you deliberately seek out.
REFLECTION	A non-judgmental look back at what happened in the learning experience. This vital stage can be achieved quite quickly without seriously disrupting the work activity.
CONCLUSION	Drawing conclusions from the thoughts and notes made at the review stage, to identify the lessons learned.
PLAN	Planning and testing the lessons learned from the conclusions, so that they can be related and applied to similar situations in the future.

Peter Honey and Alan Mumford are acknowledged experts and influential thinkers on the topic of learning styles. They identified four learning styles linked to the learning cycle and characterised them as follows:

Activists (experience)

● Open-minded people, not sceptical. This attitude tends to make them enthusiastic about everything new.

■ Their philosophy is *I'll try anything once*; they tend to act first and consider the consequences afterwards.

▲ They fill their days with activity; they tackle problems by brainstorming.

If you feel that you fit this description, then you are likely to learn best from activities where:

○ it is appropriate to 'have a go'

☐ you get involved in short activities such as role-plays, and where you have the limelight

△ you are thrown in at the deep end

○ there is a lot of excitement and a range of changing tasks to tackle, usually involving people.

Reflectors (reflection)

● Like to stand back and consider experiences, observing them from many different perspectives and listening to others before making their own comment.

■ The thorough collection and analysis of data about experiences and events is what counts, so they tend to postpone reaching definitive conclusions for as long as possible.

▲ When they act it is as part of a larger picture that includes the past as well as the present, and others' observations as well as their own.

If you fit this description then you are likely to learn best from situations where:

○ you can stand back from events and listen and observe

□ you can carry out research or analysis

△ you can decide in your own time, and have the chance to think before acting

○ you have the opportunity to review what you have learned.

Theorists (conclusion)

● Adapt and integrate observations into complex but logically sound theories, thinking through problems in a step-by-step way.

■ Tend to be perfectionists who are uncomfortable unless things are tidy and fit into a rational scheme.

▲ Are keen on basic assumptions, principles, theories, models and systems thinking.

If you feel you are a theorist you are likely to learn best when:

○ you are intellectually stretched – eg through being allowed to question assumptions or logic

□ the situation has a structure and clear purpose

△ you can deal with logical, rational argument, which you have time to explore

○ you are offered interesting concepts, although they might not be immediately relevant.

Pragmatists (plan)

● Are keen on trying out theories, ideas and techniques to see whether they work in practice.

■ Positively search out new ideas and take the first opportunity to experiment.

▲ Like to get on with things and act quickly and confidently on ideas, being impatient with extensive discussion.

As a pragmatist, you are likely to learn best from situations where you can:

○ use techniques with obvious practical benefits

☐ implement what you have learned immediately

△ try out and practise techniques

○ see an obvious link between the subject matter and a real problem or opportunity at work.

Many people have found these Honey and Mumford learning preference types both helpful and simple to apply. So let's explore a little deeper into their analysis.

Activity 8   What is your preference?

Having read through the preference characteristics, try to identify which set of characteristics most closely reflects the way you prefer to approach a learning experience. If it helps, recall a recent learning experience you felt was successful for you and use this as an example while you consider which characteristics you felt or displayed.

I feel my preferred learning style might be:

A successful learning experience where I adopted this style was:

We are not suggesting that people cannot learn from situations that do not suit their preference, but experience has shown that people learn more effectively if they can choose learning opportunities which suit their preferred learning style(s).

Your knowledge of these learning styles will help you to:

● recognise your preferred learning styles and those of your colleagues

■ design or seek out learning opportunities that will suit your preferred learning style

▲ focus on developing your least preferred styles so that you can make the most of the learning cycle.

Learning is most effective when you go through the whole learning cycle. This makes it important to develop each of these learning styles, so that you can successfully adapt your style of learning to take advantage of each stage in the cycle.

Many people have found that recognising their own style is one of the most revealing and powerful pieces of information they can obtain. It often helps to explain many earlier problems with learning and gaining qualifications and, of course, it helps to highlight the differences between colleagues and friends both in terms of learning and also in how they prefer to work.

To find out more accurately about your preferred learning style you can use the Network Helpline (Chapter 7).

Where and when

Once you have an idea of your own learning preferences you can use this information to help make good choices about where and when you might find learning easiest. There are opportunities to learn at home, in social situations, in community activities, at work, at college, through the Church, in sport and in many other places. Your ability to learn how to manage change at work, for example, is just as likely to develop through your helping out at a local playgroup as it is on a 'managing change' workshop.

Similarly, learning on training courses in the workplace is now widely recognised as only one of at least 50 ways to learn.

One of the most potent opportunities arises when things go wrong. Rather than treat mistakes as an occasion to blame, punish, hide or fail to own up, it is far more effective to treat them as learning opportunities. Everyone makes mistakes from time to time, but viewing them positively contributes to a healthy learning culture for everyone involved.

Training courses are still relevant where given procedures exist, where rules need to be adopted and where the world is unlikely to change too fast. Your own training department is an obvious first port of call. But Government agencies such as Training and Enterprise Councils (TECs) often offer a comprehensive, and usually free, guide to local opportunities. So use them!

Outside these situations, learning can take place anywhere, any time – in meetings, at presentations, at the coffee machine, across the Internet, while reading an article, planning a project, organising an outing – indeed, just about anywhere. The secret is to become much more aware of the opportunities to learn.

The great news is that teachers and trainers are everywhere too! For example, it is not uncommon when you join an organisation to learn more through the receptionist about how it works than you could ever learn on the official induction programme!

Bosses are a fabulous source of learning too, in terms of either how to do things or how not to do them. Bouncing ideas off colleagues, swapping roles with suppliers at meetings, designing an event with the customer, asking for feedback at the end of the meeting you chaired – it's all learning.

Activity 9   Learning opportunities

To help you to start thinking more widely, why not choose from the following opportunities one for you to learn at work and one for you to learn out of work? (If you are currently unemployed, try at least two anyway!) Give some thought to what you want to learn and how – either now or in the future – it will add to your earning power. Remember, only choose one or more that you can fit in comfortably with your existing life-style pressures.

- Select a radio or TV programme in your field of interest to listen to or watch next week, and then arrange to discuss it with a friend or colleague.

- Go to a local bookshop and choose a book on any topic that interests you. Read it as soon as you can and, once again, discuss the most important messages with a friend or colleague.

- Ask a friend whether it would be possible to visit his or her place of work and spend a morning alongside him or her. Write a brief report for yourself on what you found most interesting.

- Choose an evening course from the list that you will find at the nearest college, library or adult education centre.

- Organise a society, club or simple discussion group in an area of professional interest to meet at lunchtimes or immediately after work.

- If at work, think whose job you would most like to do and approach both that person and your boss to see whether it would be possible to do a job-swap for a short time.

- Explore the availability of any video or interactive computer learning programs that could be installed on your PC at work or borrowed for use at home.

- Choose a voluntary organisation and offer to work for them on Saturday mornings.

- Ask someone you know who is a specialist in a particular field to teach you the basics of his or her expertise.

- Start to keep a 'learning diary' in which you make a note each week of something specific that you have learned. Use examples both of things that have gone well and mistakes.

- Visit the local library and borrow a set of cassettes in an area of your interest – listen to them one evening rather than watching TV!

These are just 11 thought-starters. The secret is to use your imagination to think of many more and therefore start to develop the attitude 'I can learn something new every day if I just take the trouble to think about it.'

In the Network Helpline (Chapter 7) you can find other sources to help you decide what learning opportunities really work for you.

Head and heart

Before we leave this chapter there is a final thought to consider. Taking responsibility for your own learning means learning at the level of both the head and the heart.

Knowing what you *think* about an issue is only half of the story; in other words, you have only learned half of what there is to learn. Understanding how you *feel* about an issue is the second half. Knowing what you think without understanding how you feel is like trying to eat a meal with your intellect: you won't know what it tastes like and you certainly won't be full!

Getting into the habit of treating yourself as a whole person will enhance your learning. Regularly asking yourself such questions as 'How do I feel about this issue?' and, more important still, 'Why do I feel this way?' is a good discipline to develop your self-awareness and understanding, which together form a basic building-block for someone serious about learning. Remember, 'learning has to have an emotional content because learning starts in that part of the brain.'

Reflection point

Once again we suggest that you pause to think about the issues discussed in this chapter and how they may affect you. Is there something that you feel you may wish to commit yourself to doing as soon as possible? If the answer is yes, then why not write down when you will start and the date by which you hope to have completed it. But only write it down if you really intend to do it!

taking responsibility for 'learning for earning'

What may be done at any time will be done at no time.

Scottish proverb

So far you have looked at where you are starting from, how to think in different ways about the challenges you face and, in the last chapter, about how learning might be easiest for you. By now you will have an appreciation of the route you might take to fill the gaps in your skills and knowledge 'tool-kit'.

But how is all this learning going to happen? How are you actually going to get from where you are now to where you have decided you need to be? Like everything else in life, you have to decide to make it happen for yourself. *You* have to make the choice: learn or not learn.

How much do you value yourself? Do you believe that you have a right to learn? Do you believe that you deserve the opportunity to learn? Do you really believe that you need to learn in order to keep earning in the future? As the popular song puts it, do you 'really, really, really want' to make this happen?

Your answers to these questions will give you a strong indication as to whether you are going to accept responsibility for making this happen.

A closer look at responsibility

So, what does 'taking responsibility' really mean? Let's start by having a closer look at the word 'responsibility' by splitting it into its component parts: 'ability' and 'response'.

The *ability to respond* to a situation, person or event is a gift possessed by every individual. If you have never thought about the word this way before, you may need to think this one through. Accepting responsibility means accepting that you have the power to choose how you wish to respond to any situation. This concept is at the centre of personal empowerment and is critical to the level of success you are likely to achieve in life, let alone in managing your learning.

There are some simple, but linked, equations here:

- The level of responsibility you accept over your situation = the level of control you feel.

- The level of control you feel = the level of personal freedom you experience.

- ▲ The level of personal freedom you experience = the degree of happiness you enjoy in your life and therefore in your work.

You certainly have the choice to allow things to get you down. You can decide to give up trying if you do not succeed quickly. You can choose to believe that something is impossible for you to learn or achieve. The point is that *you* are responsible for the way you choose to respond to anything and everything that happens in your life.

You may not always be able to control what happens to you, but you always have a choice about how you respond.

The first step to successful personal development is to take responsibility for your life, your work and your learning.

Deciding how to spend your time

Time is the one thing that most people today wish they had more of. The work you may already do, your family, chores and household responsibilities, friends, neighbours, duties in the community etc all call upon your time. There is always the possibility of leisure time (remote as it may be beginning to seem) – for sport, the pub, the cinema, the garden... The list goes on, and that's even before you have had time to consider yourself and your future.

For some people, the idea of putting their needs in front of those of family, work and friends, even for a short while, constitutes selfishness beyond redemption. But you are going to have to foster a degree of healthy selfishness if you want to improve your lot for both yourself and your loved ones. Charles Handy calls it 'proper selfishness' in his 1997 book

The Hungry Spirit. How can you begin to look after the future of others if you are not first looking after your own?

How much time do you currently spend examining and meeting your own needs? An even more fundamental equation is relevant here:

Looking after yourself and satisfying your own needs some of the time

$$= \text{HEALTH}.$$

Looking after the needs and wants of others and never taking time for yourself

$$= \text{BREAKDOWN}.$$

Reflection point

This question of 'proper selfishness' is another important lesson in managing your own learning. You are going to have to decide what you will relinquish in order to take time to learn. Take some time to note down the things you could stop doing that would give you time to spend on your learning.

Staying disciplined

Just like anything else new in your routine, staying focused and on track requires discipline. As we have discussed, your determination to succeed depends on a number of things but, predominantly, on how inspired you are by your vision of what your learning will bring you and what you have to lose by not succeeding.

Let's have a look first at your vision.

The work you have done in the earlier chapters should have provided you with a clear picture of what it is you are trying to achieve. It may be as straightforward as mastering a skill, taking on a new job or learning to speak French. Whatever it is, the clearer you are about how life will be for you when you have achieved it, the higher your levels of motivation are likely to be. If it is a new job, for example, ask yourself whether you have spent time visualising how life will be for you in this new role. If you have not, take some time now to imagine yourself doing this new job.

Activity 11 Your vision

Take yourself off to a place where you are comfortable and unlikely to be disturbed, close your eyes, relax, take a few deep breaths and take 10 minutes to think through the answers to the following questions:

- How do you see yourself in this new/ideal job?
- What are you doing?

- ▲ Whom are you talking to?
- ◉ What are you saying?
- ◉ How are you dressed?
- ◉ Where are you working?
- ◻ What is the environment like?
- ▲ Are you alone or with people?
- ◉ How are you feeling?
- ◉ What is pleasing you?
- ◉ What are your family and friends thinking and feeling?

After the 10 minutes are over, jot down your answers. Are you inspired or bored by the picture you have just created?

It is a good idea to continue to practise seeing yourself in your new situation. It will help you to refine your vision further and to re-inforce your commitment to it. The more real you make it, the more possible it will seem. The questions above will also help you to understand everything you have to gain by succeeding in learning in your chosen field. The more you desire your vision, the more likely you are to remain committed and disciplined.

Getting organised

Without doubt, a major hindrance to many people in managing their own learning is simply a lack of personal organisation.

There are a number of questions for you to consider which may help you here:

● Where will your learning take place? At home, in the library, in a class, everywhere? If at home, where will you study, contemplate, write, create, etc? Be clear and honest with yourself and then write down your answers to re-inforce your decisions.

▪ How effective is your learning likely to be in the place you have chosen? What will the hindrances or distractions be, and how can you minimise them? Remember what we said about healthy selfishness. You may need to be very tough with yourself to make the best use of precious time.

▲ How will you keep records and files of contacts, articles, tips, telephone numbers? Do you need a computer? Do you need help to create a filing system on your computer? Do you need to get some basic computing skills before you start? Is it worth revisiting earlier sections of this book where you have already reflected on some of these issues? It is difficult to imagine, for instance, that people will not be making increased use of the Internet to help find new information and ideas. For those with little or no knowledge of computers this is likely to become a learning need. But there really is a great deal of help available if only you are prepared to ask for it.

● Do you have enough, or the right, information at this stage? Before you begin to invest your time and energy into your learning, it is worth checking that you have all the information you need. Asking a coach, friend or partner to ask you all the questions they can think of relating to your chosen field of learning is a good way to test your level of preparation.

● Are you sure that your end goal is clear? Do you find your end goal motivating and inspirational? If your end goal is unclear or, worse still, clear but uninspiring, you may find it tough when you face the occasional obstacle.

Having an end goal is vital, but it is sensible to break that down into a series of shorter-term goals. The pace at which things change can sometimes make an end goal seem impossible to reach. Development goals that have a three- to four-month timescale are often much more achievable. A personal development plan (PDP) is an effective way of maintaining your focus. Reviewing it monthly to monitor progress and make any adjustments will help to keep you on track.

● Are you spending time reflecting on your experiences? Keeping a learning log regularly can be a helpful way of maintaining your energy for learning. And, for those who are Activists or Pragmatists, it is a useful reminder that effective learning requires *all* stages of the learning cycle to be used.

Finally, a word of caution. Don't attempt to do too much too quickly. Better by far to tackle one learning need properly over the next three months than to try to fill every gap within a 12-month programme. A series of small steps results in faster and more reliable progress than trying to do everything in one giant stride.

Reflection point

If you feel that managing your time in a more disciplined way and concentrating on becoming really well organised will be a problem for you, would it help to talk to someone you know who manages both these things quite well? Do they have any tips or techniques that you could use? Or is it simply a case that you don't want to succeed sufficiently strongly? Pause to make a note or two before we discuss these issues in the next chapter.

If one advances confidently in the direction of his dreams, and endeavours to live the life which he has imagined, he will meet with success unexpected in common hours.

Henry David Thoreau

Success has a great deal to do with developing self-confidence and self-belief, as well as taking self-responsibility.

A very important ingredient for building self-confidence is to realise that it is a mistake to think that 'self-responsibility = solo responsibility'. You very rarely need to tackle the challenges of analysing your needs, developing your plan and monitoring your progress all on your own. You will be surprised how willing people are to help, especially when they recognise someone with a clear determination to maximise their potential and improve their performance.

Asking someone to act as your coach or mentor could be the best decision you take. It is better still, without doubt, simultaneously to offer to be a coach or mentor to someone else.

The insights you will gain into the process, the pressures, and the highs and lows of tackling the challenges by sharing the learning journey with someone else will almost certainly bolster your self-confidence and motivation to maintain your own learning momentum. Self-confidence and personal motivation are two of the essentials for success.

Although teaching is very different from coaching and mentoring, the value of helping others to learn as a way of helping yourself is captured in two quite well-known quotations:

Thoroughly to teach another is the best way to teach yourself.

Tryon Edwards

To teach is to learn twice.

Joseph Joubert

You may feel that coaching and mentoring are too time-consuming for you or your colleagues to consider while you yourself are learning. But you would be wrong.

Keep it simple

It takes time, and of course a lot of practice, to become an 'expert' coach and mentor. There are a lot of good books on the theory, techniques and skills that will help you. But most people can become proficient quite quickly. Remember the story of the tortoise and the hare? As we put it, 'success comes most surely by doing simple things consistently'.

At its basic level, a coaching and mentoring session is simply a one-to-one meeting aimed at helping the person receiving the coaching and mentoring to learn how he or she can best improve performance at work or in his or her personal life.

These meetings should happen regularly. Keeping a learning diary is the simplest way of planning to make this happen. The agenda for the meetings has to be determined entirely by the person on the receiving end. The coach and mentor should add items to the agenda only by making suggestions. The meetings, even brief informal ones, work best with a written agenda and a coach or mentor who ensures that that agenda is completed on time!

It is useful sometimes to keep a note of the issues discussed. But it is more important for both parties to keep a record of the action points that are decided upon during the session. These will result in real action only if they are truly owned by the person being coached or mentored. They then become the first item for review at the next session.

This simple, regular structure is the basis of successful coaching and mentoring. Although some people may find the structured and disciplined approach uncomfortable, both parties usually benefit.

Keep it focused

As we have said already, the focus of the session should be on the person who wishes to improve performance, even if it is a joint learning experience. The coach and mentor will typically spend about 80 per cent of the session simply listening and asking questions. For the rest of the time, he or she may be making suggestions to help the other person work out for him- or herself what needs doing. Occasionally it is useful to tell or instruct. But if the coach and mentor is spending more than 5 per cent of the time doing this, he or she is probably getting it wrong.

As we advocated earlier, a series of short, manageable steps is often the fastest way to make real progress. As you can see, the process of concentrating on the needs of a fellow learner highlights many of the issues that apply to your own situation.

Fundamentals check-list

It is time to summarise the ideas and experiences we have shared with you in this book. It would be nice to be able to say, 'Well, there you are then: just follow this model and success will be yours.' Unfortunately, there are no easy answers or solutions. Your route will apply only to you. However, our final check-list comprises what we believe are the seven fundamentals for 'learning for earning':

- Do I really believe that I have both a need and a desire to learn?

- Have I analysed and prioritised my learning needs at both a practical and personal level to help me become the person that I could be?

▲ Have I started to think differently about the choices I can make in order to tackle the learning challenges ahead?

◉ Do I understand how to match my learning-style preferences to the opportunities available to me in order to make my learning more enjoyable and therefore easier and quicker?

◉ Do I accept that I alone can choose to take responsibility for having a disciplined approach to managing the time that it will take to complete my learning journey?

◉ Do I recognise the value of helping someone else to succeed as a means of helping myself to succeed as well?

▣ Do I accept that I do not need to make the process complicated, because success will come most surely by doing simple things consistently?

We hope that you can say yes to each of these questions, at least with some conviction. In this book we have shared our ideas and some of the techniques that have proved helpful both to us and many others in similar circumstances. Not all of our suggestions will necessarily work for you. Indeed, not all of them are necessary for everyone. We hope, however, that we have helped point you in the direction you wish, and choose, to travel on your learning journey.

Good luck! We hope you arrive safely.

7 the network helpline

A key principle that we have advocated throughout this book is that knowing where to go to access information is more important than trying to keep information in your head. Our knowledge of how the brain works tells us that even after a stimulating learning experience (like reading this book, we hope!), only a small percentage of the information will remain in our short-term memory and that without repetition and re-inforcement even less will move reliably into our long-term memory. This Network Helpline is intended to give you the opportunity to revisit some of the ideas and suggestions in an interesting way to encourage the information to remain active and useful.

The Network Helpline is intended also to give you access to additional information on the topics we have discussed. It is organised by chapters for easy reference.

Chapter 1

The web-site of the Institute of Personnel and Development is a source of a host of relevant information. Visiting www.ipd.co.uk will allow you to read more about:

- the *Declaration on Learning* by Peter Honey *et al*, published in *People Management* 1 October 1998

- the 'Rushing revolution' by Margaret Malpas, published in *People Management* 17 September 1998

▲ the full range of IPD Books: telephone 0181 263 3387 or e-mail publish@ipd.co.uk. Among the books published by the IPD we would draw particular attention to:

  ○ *Get More from Work – and More Fun* by Neasa MacErlean (1998)

  □ *Learning Alliances: Tapping into talent* by David Clutterbuck (1998)

  △ *Cultivating Self-Development* by David Megginson and Vivien Whitaker (1996).

There is a number of Government agencies that provide comprehensive (and usually free) advice on issues related to learning and employment. A good place to start your enquiries would be the Department for Education and Employment (DfEE): telephone 0845 602 2260 or e-mail dfee@prologistics.co.uk.

Chapter 2

Here are some suggestions for more information on personality-profiling:

- the British Psychological Society: telephone 0116 254 9580 or e-mail enquiries@bps.org.uk

- ®MBTI and Myers-Briggs Type Indicator are registered UK and US trademarks of Consulting Psychology Press Inc. Oxford Psychologists Press Ltd is the exclusive licensee of the trademark in the UK: telephone 01865 510203 or e-mail enquiry@opp.co.uk

- ▲ For information on enneagrams and various networks contact Julie Hay via the Association of Management Education and Development by telephoning 0171 235 3505 or e-mailing enquiries@adinternational.com.

Chapter 3

The following publications should prove stimulating:

- Stephen Covey and Roger Merrill, *First Things First* from Simon and Schuster ISBN 0-671-71283-2 or The Covey Leadership Centre, telephone 0121 604 6999 or e-mail unitedkingdom@covey.com

- Brian Tracey, *The Psychology of Achievement* (six audiocassettes) published by Nightingale-Conant ISBN 1555253527

- ▲ Nancy Kline, *Time to Think – Listening to ignite the human mind* from Cassell ISBN 0-7063-7745-1.

Chapter 4

Additional reading on the theory and practice of learning includes:

- Peter Honey and Alan Mumford, *Learning Style Preferences*, published by Peter Honey ISBN 0 950844 1 1. Telephone 01628 633946 or e-mail peterhoney@peterhoney.co.uk

- Jenny Maddern, *Accelerated Learning*, published by the Accelerated Learning Centre; telephone 01267 211880 or e-mail books@anglo-american.co.uk

One of many useful networks to consider joining is 'The Learning Network' at Wolsey Hall, Oxford; telephone 01865 310 310 or website www.wolseyhall.co.uk

Chapter 5

Ideas and techniques to help take control of your learning can be found in:

- Stephen Covey, *Seven Habits of Highly Effective People*, published by Simon and Schuster ISBN 0-671-71117-2 at the same contact address as above.

- *SMILE* (Self-Managed Integrated Learning), a 'tool-kit' published by Wolsey Hall, Oxford at the same contact address as above.

▲ Andrew Forrest, *Fifty Ways to Personal Development*, published by the Industrial Society; telephone 0171 262 2401 or e-mail infoserv@indusoc.demon.co.uk

Chapter 6

Material to provide extra information on helping others to learn can be obtained from:

● *Mentoring*, a CD-Rom published by the Sutton Regeneration Partnership and the London Borough of Sutton; telephone 0181 770 4641 or e-mail raynert@sutton.gov.uk

■ the Oxford School of Coaching and Mentoring; telephone 01865 310 310 or e-mail oscm@wolseyhall.co.uk

▲ *Self-Managed Learning*, a guide to best practice published by the Industrial Society, at the same contact address as above.

With over 90,000 members, the **Institute of Personnel and Development** is the largest organisation in Europe dealing with the management and development of people. The IPD operates its own publishing unit, producing books and research reports for human resource practitioners, students, and general managers charged with people-management responsibilities.

Currently there are over 160 titles covering the full range of personnel and development issues. The books have been commissioned from leading experts in the field and are packed with the latest information and guidance on best practice.

For free copies of the IPD Books Catalogue, please contact the publishing department:

Tel.: 0181-263 3387
Fax: 0181-263 3850
E-mail: publish@ipd.co.uk
Web: http://www.ipd.co.uk

Orders for books should be sent to:

Plymbridge Distributors
Estover
Plymouth
Devon
PL6 7PZ

(Credit card orders) Tel.: 01752 202 301
Fax: 01752 202 333

Upcoming titles in the *Management Shapers* series

Publication: March 1999

Body Language at Work
Adrian Furnham
ISBN 0 85292 771 1

Introducing NLP
Sue Knight
ISBN 0 85292 772 X

Other titles in the *Management Shapers* series

All titles are priced at £5.95 (£5.36 to IPD members)

The Appraisal Discussion

Terry Gillen

Shows you how to make appraisal a productive and motivating experience for all levels of performer. It includes:

- assessing performance fairly and accurately

- using feedback to improve performance

- handling reluctant appraisees and avoiding bias

- agreeing future objectives

- identifying development needs.

1998 96 pages   ISBN 0 85292 751 7

Asking Questions

Ian MacKay
(Second Edition)

Will help you ask the 'right' questions, using the correct form to elicit a useful response. All managers need to hone their questioning skills, whether interviewing, appraising or simply exchanging ideas. This book offers guidance and helpful advice on:

- using various forms of open question – including probing, simple interrogative, opinion-seeking, hypothetical, extension and precision etc

- encouraging and drawing out speakers through supportive statements and interjections

- establishing specific facts through closed or 'direct' approaches

- avoiding counter-productive questions

- using questions in a training context.

1998 96 pages   ISBN 0 85292 768 1

Assertiveness

Terry Gillen

Will help you feel naturally confident, enjoy the respect of others and easily establish productive working relationships, even with 'awkward' people. It covers:

- understanding why you behave as you do and, when that behaviour is counter-productive, knowing what to do about it

- understanding other people better

- keeping your emotions under control

- preventing others' bullying, flattering or manipulating you

- acquiring easy-to-learn techniques that you can use immediately

- developing your personal assertiveness strategy.

1998 96 pages   ISBN 0 85292 769 X

Constructive Feedback

Roland and Frances Bee

Practical advice on when to give feedback, how best to give it, and how to receive and use feedback yourself. It includes:

- using feedback in coaching, training, and team motivation
- distinguishing between criticism and feedback
- 10 tools for giving constructive feedback
- dealing with challenging situations and people.

1998 96 pages   ISBN 0 85292 752 5

The Disciplinary Interview

Alan Fowler

This book will ensure that you adopt the correct procedures, conduct productive interviews and manage the outcome with confidence. It includes:

- understanding the legal implications
- investigating the facts and presenting the management case
- probing the employee's case and defusing conflict
- distinguishing between conduct and competence
- weighing up the alternatives to dismissal.

1998 96 pages   ISBN 0 85292 753 3

Leadership Skills

John Adair

Will give you confidence and guide and inspire you on your journey from being an effective manager to becoming a leader of excellence. Acknowledged as a world authority on leadership, Adair offers stimulating insights into:

- recognising and developing your leadership qualities

- acquiring the personal authority to give positive direction and the flexibility to embrace change

- acting on the key interacting needs – to achieve your task, build your team, and develop its members

- transforming the core leadership functions such as planning, communicating and motivating into practical skills you can master.

1998 96 pages   ISBN 0 85292 764 9

Listening Skills

Ian MacKay
(Second Edition)

Improve your ability in this crucial management skill! Clear explanations will help you:

- recognise the inhibitors to listening

- listen to what is really being said by analysing and evaluating the message

- interpret tone of voice and non-verbal signals.

1998 80 pages   ISBN 0 85292 754 1

Making Meetings Work

Patrick Forsyth

Will maximise your time (both before and during meetings), clarify your aims, improve your own and others' performance and make the whole process rewarding and productive. The book is full of practical tips and advice on:

- drawing up objectives and setting realistic agendas

- deciding the who, where, and when to meet

- chairing effectively – encouraging discussion, creativity and sound decision-making

- sharpening your skills of observation, listening and questioning to get your points across

- dealing with problem participants

- handling the follow-up – turning decisions into action.

1998 96 pages   ISBN 0 85292 765 7

Motivating People

Iain Maitland

Will help you maximise individual and team skills to achieve personal, departmental and, above all, organisational goals. It provides practical insights into:

- becoming a better leader and co-ordinating winning teams

- identifying, setting and communicating achievable targets

- empowering others through simple job improvement techniques

- encouraging self-development, defining training needs and providing helpful assessment

- ensuring that pay and workplace conditions make a positive contribution to satisfaction and commitment.

1998 96 pages   ISBN 0 85292 766 5

Negotiating, Persuading and Influencing

Alan Fowler

Develop the skills you need to manage your staff effectively, bargain successfully with colleagues or deal tactfully with superiors. Sound advice on:

- probing and questioning techniques

- timing your tactics and using adjournments

- conceding and compromising to find common ground

- resisting manipulative ploys

- securing and implementing agreement.

1998 96 pages   ISBN 085292 755 X